The Jewel Tower

WESTMINSTER

A J TAYLOR CBE, MA, DLitt, FSA, FRHist S

The Jewel Tower, situated opposite the houses of Parliament, was once part of the Medieval Palace of Westminster and its story is closely connected with that of British government.

This L-shaped, three storey building of white Kentish stone has survived many fires and floods. It sits squarely in the south-west corner of Old Palace Yard where it was built in 1365 as a personal treasure-house for Edward III and known as the King's Privy Wardrobe.

The Tower was used by other monarchs for their personal treasure until 1621 when it was converted to house government documents. In 1869 it underwent another transformation to become the official Weights and Measures office.

As well as having a fascinating history, the building is of great architectural interest, containing an unrestored fourteenth century ribbed vault comparable in quality to the similar vaults in the cloister of Westminster Abbey. There are also several original window embrasures and a fourteenth century door on the second floor.

The guidebook gives a detailed history of the tower and describes its architectural features with the use of photographs, reproduced documents and new plans.

ENGLISH HERITAGE · LONDON

Contents

Published by English Heritage
1 Waterhouse Square, 138-142 Holborn, London EC1N 2ST
© Copyright English Heritage 1996, reprinted 2001, 2005, 2006, 2007
Printed in England by Matthews The Printers Ltd
07054 C30 11/07
ISBN 1 85074 643 5
www.english-heritage.org.uk

Introduction

From the reign of Edward the Confessor (1042-66) until the early part of that of Henry the Eighth (1509-47) the kings of England had their principal residence at Westminster. Its site is today largely occupied by the Houses of Parliament, still officially named the Palace of Westminster. In the course of a history extending over nine centuries, its buildings have undergone many vicissitudes, and on at least three occasions (1298, 1512 and 1834) large parts of them suffered destruction by fire. Nevertheless, several parts of the medieval palace still remain today. The greatest and most famous of these is Westminster Hall, dating in its present form from the time of Richard II (1377-99) but incorporating in its walls substantial parts of the great hall originally built by William Rufus (1087-1100). To the south-east of the hall stands the early fourteenth-century crypt chapel of St Mary Undercroft restored after the fire of 1834 had destroyed its upper storey, the collegiate chapel of St Stephen, which had served since 1547 as the meeting place of the House of Commons and the site of which is now occupied by St Stephen's Hall. In the angle between it and Westminster Hall are the Cloisters, also largely rebuilt after the fire of 1834 and again after war-damage in 1940, but originally erected between 1525 and 1530 to serve St Stephen's.

Least known, yet in some respects least altered and by no means the least interesting of the survivals of the medieval palace, is the building called the Jewel Tower. Alone of all of them it retains externally its walls of white Kentish rag, to remind us, like the later Water Tower

(1434-35) of Lambeth Palace across the river, of the lighter colouring once characteristic of all the Westminster buildings. It is also the only one to have, within, an unrestored fourteenth-century ribbed vault, comparable in quality with the contemporary vaults in the nearby Abbey cloister. Even the position of the Jewel Tower, standing apart as it does from Westminster Hall and the main group of buildings beside the Thames, is a matter of interest. It recalls the fact that the medieval palace extended right to this point, the tower having actually been built so as to embrace, and indeed to encroach a little beyond, its extreme south-west corner. From the beginning, that is to say from the Confessor's time, the southern part of the estate was occupied by the private palace, and the Jewel Tower, as we shall see, was essentially built to serve purposes to do with the King's private household. When, in the last years of the eleventh century, Rufus built his great new hall, it in fact represented a northward extension away from the Confessor's original nucleus, the main courtyard of which began from that time to be known as the "Old" Palace Yard. By the middle of the fourteenth century, when the Jewel Tower was built, the private palace on the south was regarded as something separate and apart from the northern buildings. These, having by then become the regular meeting-place of the Courts of King's Bench, Common Pleas, Exchequer and Chancery and the home of the College of St Stephen, were necessarily places of public resort. Within the private palace itself the principal buildings, including the old or lesser White Hall, the Painted Chamber and the

Prince's Chamber, lay to the south and east of the "Old" Yard, but others, most of them destroyed in the fire of 1512, lay with the King's privy garden to the south and west of it. Of these last, as indeed of the private palace as a whole, the Jewel Tower is the sole survivor. Long obscured from view, it has now regained something of its former status as an integral part of the Palace of Westminster following post-war clearance of later houses in Abingdon Street and Old Palace Yard.

The Jewel Tower and moat from the south-east

History

1365-66 Site, design and construction

The story of the construction of the Jewel Tower can be recovered with some precision from a number of contemporary and near-contemporary records. Chief among these is a closely written 8½ ft long parchment account roll, preserved in the Public Record Office, on which are summarised details of expenditure on materials, carriage and wages laid out in the construction not of one but of two new towers which were both being built within the Palace of Westminster during the later months of the year 1365 and the spring and summer of 1366. One of them, a Clock Tower (it was pulled down in 1698 but its appearance is known from one of Hollar's engravings), stood on the north side of New Palace Yard a little to the west of where the present clock tower stands; the latter was built nearly 500 years later and it houses the bell, Big Ben.

The other, the Jewel Tower, is variously referred to in the account as "the new tower beside, or on the edge of, the King's garden," or "in the angle of the King's privy palace". These descriptions are literally correct, for the tower's L-shaped plan was purposely devised to enclose the south-west corner of the palace ground without actually impinging on it. This meant, however, that the greater part of the tower, and the whole of the moat and "close" which surrounded its outer sides, had in fact to be build on the land of the Crown's next-door neighbours, the abbot and convent of St Peter's, Westminster. Not until 1372, six years after the tower was finished, did the Abbey obtain permission to acquire

(at their own expense) other lands in compensation, and it was another twenty years after that before they were able to complete their purchases.

The compiler of the Liber Niger, the late fifteenth-century Register or Chartulary preserved among the Abbey muniments, leaves us in no doubt that the monks bitterly resented this encroachment on the soil of St Peter, and recounts with unconcealed delight the fate that overtook the royal official they regarded as its instigator. This was a certain William Ussheborne, who in the 1350s and '60s held the office of Keeper of the King's Privy Palace, a post today vested with other ancient keeperships in the Department of the Environment. He it was, says the chronicler, who acquired, for the King's use, a close that belonged by rights to the Prior of Westminster and had a garden and a fishpond built there which he stocked with fresh-water fish. But not long afterwards he chanced to invite some Westminster friends to dinner, and served as the principal dish a pike from this very pond. No sooner had they all begun to eat than the wretched Ussheborne started to cry out that the pike was choking him, and, lo and behold, in but a little while he was a dead man without absolution. Such, writes the chronicler, was the end of one who, besides misappropriating this garden of the prior's, was also said to be behind the loss of a field and garden belonging to the Infirmarer: clearly it was only thanks to his office that he secured immediate burial in the choir of St Margaret's! The story is worth the telling, particularly because, in the fullness of time, Ussheborne's fishpond, which was in fact

Reconstruction painting of the garden and fishpond created by the Keeper of the King's Privy Palace for Edward III's use between 1350 and 1370 in the L-shape of the Jewel Tower.

none other than the moat of the Jewel Tower, with the little close or garden beside it, has lately been once more revealed to sight.

There is little doubt that the tower was designed by Henry de Yevele, "deviser of the King's works of masonry" and the most famous architect of his day. Yevele's name heads the list of payments to masons (see page 14) who worked on both the "tower for the clock" and "the tower by the King's garden", and he is said to be responsible for "obtaining their work". He also received individual payments for supplying plaster of Paris for rendering the floor of the Jewel Tower and 7000 bricks ("Flanders tiles") for paving floors and other works. The main carpentry construction for both towers

was "ordained" by Hugh Herland, later famous as the creator of Westminster Hall roof, but at this time still working under his father, Master William.

The bulk of the building stone was Kentish rag, of which ninety-eight boat-loads were shipped from Maidstone to Westminster for the two towers. For the dressings - doors, windows and battlements - Reigate stone was used: this was carried by cart (469 loads) from Reigate to Battersea, whence it was shipped downstream to Westminster in fifty-three barges. Beer stone from Devon (26 tons) and Caen stone from Normandy (16 tons) was used for the string courses of both towers and for the gargoyles of the Jewel Tower. The ashlar stone needed for the building (8107ft) and 5675ft of urnell (a more roughly dressed stone) were obtained from Maidstone. For the circular wall of the Jewel Tower staircase, 240 specially cut stones called "sherches", costing 4d apiece, were bought at Reigate. Timber was likewise procured from a variety of places in Surrey and brought to Westminster by river from Kingston or Lambeth. Ninety-seven feet of white glass, worked with flowers and with the royal arms in the borders, was bought for the Jewel Tower windows. All of these, the three large ones facing east into the palace garden together with ten smaller ones, were protected externally by heavy wrought-iron grilles, the fixing of which was done by a contractor, Thomas Hardegrey, who also had a general contract of £60 "for making the aforesaid Tower next the King's garden."

The accounts do not allow us to trace the progress of the building stage by stage, though one or two operations are closely dated. Thus we know that between the beginning of November 1365 and the end of January 1366, fifteen masons were engaged in dressing stones for the windows, crestings, chimneys and string courses, while towards the middle of the following July twenty-three navvies began the digging out of the moat, a task which they completed in ten working days. An already existing ditch between the Jewel Tower and the Thames was cleared out and connected with the new moat.

1366-1547 King's Privy Wardrobe

Jewels and plate played an important part in the economy and ceremonial of medieval England. King Edward III, who instituted the Order of the Garter in 1348 and towards the end of whose long reign (1327-77) the Jewel Tower was built, himself loved pomp and splendour and was never too poor to buy the costly vessels and rich jewellery that were the accepted trappings of a gorgeous and resplendent age.

It is necessary for our present purpose to distinguish, at the risk of some oversimplification, between three main categories of royal jewels. First there were the Regalia proper, or ceremonial Crown Jewels, those used only at Coronations being in the custody of the abbot and convent of Westminster, while there were others, worn more frequently, which were normally kept at the Tower of London. Secondly, there would as a rule be much jewellery and plate, as well as coins, in the King's treasury in Westminster Abbey (the Pyx Chamber), administered by the Treasurer and Barons of the Exchequer. Thirdly, there was the sovereign's private and personal treasure of precious stones and gold and silver ware, administered at the time of which we are speaking as a branch of the King's Privy Wardrobe at Westminster. It is with this last collection, and this alone, that we are concerned in the present context, for it was to provide secure accommodation for valuables within the personal disposal of the sovereign that the new tower at the corner of the King's garden was erected and moated round. Probably the reason for its being built at Westminster at this time is to be sought in the fact that under the stress of the French War the main Privy Wardrobe, at the Tower of London, had lately become almost exclusively concerned with the storage and distribution of military supplies and equipment.

The officer administratively responsible for the building of the Jewel Tower was the clerk and surveyor of the King's works within the Palace of Westminster and the Tower of London, a certain William of Sleaford. With his clerkship of the works this William, who was one of a family of high office holders in the fourteenth-century civil service, combined the duties of keeping the Westminster Privy Wardrobe and the dues attaching to the deanery of St Stephen's. In the first of these capacities he had charge over the contents of the building whose erection he had himself supervised as clerk of works. His brother, John of Sleaford, became Keeper of the Privy Wardrobe in the Tower of London in 1365.

Contemporary records give us a good idea of what William of Sleaford's duties were and of the kind of use to which the tower was put in the earliest years of its existence. Thus in 1369 and 1370 we have a series of writs from the King in which Sleaford, addressed as "clerk of our jewels and vessels of gold and silver within our Private Palace of Westminster," keeper of our vessels of gold and silver being in our wardrobe within our Private Palace", or even simply as "keeper of our privy wardrobe," is directed to deliver certain plate or jewels in his keeping either to named magnates or to another branch of the royal household. In 1369, for example, he was to hand to the clerk of Edmund Earl of Cambridge, one of the King's younger sons, a quantity of plate that had belonged to his elder brother Lionel, Duke of Clarence, who had died in the previous year. It included, amongst many items listed and weighed, half a dozen silver spoons marked with falcons' heads, a dozen marked with an "E" and a Crown, two silver charges having the mark of Queen Isabella, two silver mugs marked with the arms of Lionel, a pair of silver gilt basins having two escutcheons of red roses on their borders, and a silver gilt spice dish with an enamelled top and a representation of a castle and a damsel chastising a wild man of the woods (un Chastel & une damoiselle chastesante un Wodewose). Another writ required him to deliver as a gift to William Latimer,

Steward of the Household, a casket of beryl garnished with gold. Or again, William of Gunthorp, Keeper of the Wardrobe, was to receive a large consignment of plate, including seventeen dishes marked with the Walcote arms, thirteen silver spoons bearing the arms of Robert of Corby, six silver charges with the Beauchamp arms and five dishes marked with an escutcheon of leopards and fleurs-de-lys.

The Jewel Tower was the repository from which these items were distributed and into which accessions were received. Here they were weighed and assayed, their marks were listed and inventoried, and their transfer or disposal recorded by means of bipartite indentures. The tower was, in other words, an office as well as a treasure house, and its day-to-day workings may not have been very unlike those which we know from the Black Book of the Household of Edward II (1461-83) to have been followed a century later at the Jewel House in the Tower of London. There, as the Black Book tells us, "betwixt the Thesaurere of household and this office of Jewell-house, be many interchaunges of sylver vessels, whole or broke, received or delyvered by officers, by indentures. All thinges of this office inward or outward, commyth and goyth by the knowledge of the Kyng, and his chamberlaynes recorde." The same source describes the head of the Tower of London Jewel House as "clerk or keeper of the King's jewelles, or tresorer of the chambyr. This officer taketh by indenture, betwixt him and the Kinge, all that he findes in his office of gold, silver, precious stones, and the marks of every thinge. Also he receiveth the yearely guiftes by recorde of the chamberlaine". The keeper ranked as a knight. Under him, for office staff, he had a clerk, to keep the records and draw up the indentures or duplicate receipts; a yeoman, who might receive

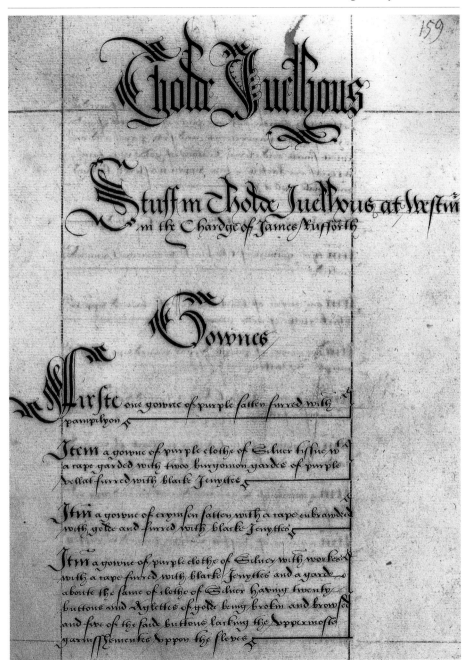

First page of Inventory of contents of the Jewel Tower in 1547, headed 'Stuff in Tholde Juelhous at Westm'(inster). (From Harleian MS 1419A, by courtesy of the Trustees of the British Museum)

"his reward of the jewel-house for trewe and diligent kepinge of the foresayd jewelles, &c"; and a groom, who kept the office, set out the candles, tended the fires (there was from the beginning a fireplace in each of the three larger rooms of the Westminster Jewel Tower) and strewed the rushes on the floor. When, as was often the case, the court was on the move, the Jewel House was assigned "a charryette with vi horses to carry the stuffe of the King's in this office," and it was the groom's task to load and guard it.

It is probable that, besides jewels and plate, the Jewel Tower also generally housed certain robes and liveries. According to the Edward IV ordinances the Eight Children of the Chapel Royal, for example, were to be "founden by the King's Jewel-house for all thinges that belongeth to thayre apparayle." Similarly we are told, with regard to the vestments, frontals, hangings and "all suche sacred stuffe of holy churche" used in the chapel, that their "purveyaunce lyeth in charge to the Kinge's warderobe and to his jewel-house." Though the ordinances are to be read as applying primarily to the Jewel House at the Tower, it is likely that they reflect the general practice of the Household and that the Westminster repository served a similar variety of uses.

These characteristic functions are likely to have been going on, with little essential change, in 1512, the year in which, as John Stow tells us, "a great part of this palace at Westminster was once again burnt...since the which time [he was writing half a century or so later] it hath not been re-edified...but the princes have been lodged in other places about the city, as at Baynarde's castle, at Bridewell, and White hall, sometime called York place, and sometime at St James." It appears that, with the removal of the court to Whitehall, the jewels and plate hitherto kept in the Jewel Tower were transferred to a "secreate Jewel-house" in the new palace. Consequently, by the end of Henry VIII's reign (1547) the Jewel Tower was already being spoken of as "Tholde Juelhous" at Westminster.

Meanwhile the tower, which from its inception had been connected with the King's Privy Wardrobe, had been turned into something very much more like a wardrobe in the modern sense of that word. An inventory of its contents (see page 9), taken immediately after Henry VIII's death, shows us that it had by then become a store, packed with every conceivable article of the late King's wearing apparel, bed linen and soft furnishings. Even the royal chessmen, the walking-sticks and the princesses' dolls had found a home here. The following items are but a few chosen at random from a list covering fifty-four pages and classified under thirty-one headings:

Item three Mantles for thordre of sainte George, twoo of blewe vellat and thother of purple vellat lyned with white Sarconet.

Item foure Shertebandes of golde, with ruffes to the same.

Item one payer of Sleves of crymsen satten, bordred with goldesmythes worke and teyed with vij payer of aglettes of golde and one odde aglett.

Item one Stomacher of white clothe of golde raised with golde and silver tissue.

Item one great steele loking glasse covered with crymsen vellat ambrawdred with damaske golde and garnished with smale perles.

Item a greate babye, lying in a boxe of wood, having a gowne of white clothe of silver and a kirtle of grene vellat, the gowne teyed with smale aglettes of golde, and a smale payer of beades of golde, and a smale cheyne and a coller aboute the necke of golde.

Item one sett of chessmen of wood in a boxe of wood, some of theym being broken.

Item one...sable skynne, with a hedd of golde

musled, garnished and sett with foure Emerades, foure turquesses, vj rubies, twoo dyamountes and v perles, with four feete of golde eche sett with a turques, the tonge being a rubye.

By 1551 the whole of this remarkable collection, some of the pieces of which had doubtless contributed their share to the magnificence of the Field of Cloth of Gold, had been sold and dispersed by command of the boy King Edward VI (1547-53). Neither under him nor under his half-sisters, Mary I (1553-58) and Elizabeth I (1558-1603), do we hear again of the Jewel Tower, but we know from a later record that during part of this period it was in the occupation of Sir Richard Shelley, the diplomat and traveller, who claimed to be the first Englishman to visit Constantinople since its capture by the Turks and who was the last Grand Prior of the Order of the Hospital of St John of Jerusalem in England. A deed of 1553 refers to it simply as "a little Tower of the old palace," and another, of 1611, makes incidental mention of it as "a Tower built upon the stonewall within the old palace of Westminster." According to a contemporary tract it was near here in Old Palace Yard that Guy Fawkes and three of his fellow-conspirators, Winter, Rockwood and Cayes, were executed on 31 January 1606, having been brought back from the Tower to pay the penalty near to the Parliament House that had been the scene of their crime. In 1620 "the Stone Tower with thappurtenaunces in the old palace yard" was let by James I to Sir William Pitt, a justice of the peace for the county of Middlesex, for a rent of ten shillings a year.

1621-1864 Parliament Office

The following year, 1621, marks a turning-point, and for the next two-and-

a-half centuries the Jewel Tower was to become the repository of contents of a totally different kind, less intrinsically valuable perhaps but with a no less high claim to safe and secure custody.

The finding of adequate accommodation for the ever mounting accumulation of government records had long been a problem at Westminster, and a variety of buildings, chief among them the great Chapter House of the Abbey, were sacrificed to its solution. As the approaching constitutional conflict cast its shadow ahead, the records of Parliament itself began both to increase their scope and to assume a new importance. In 1597 the Lords passed a motion that Journal Books of their proceedings should henceforth be kept officially and supervised by the House instead of, as hitherto, privately by the Clerk of the Parliaments. Early in 1621 they appointed a subcommittee to view and search all records necessary for considering the Customs, Orders and Privileges of the House. Later in the year, no doubt as a result of the committee's findings, the peers ordered "that the Records of this Parliament be entered and enrolled, viz. the Journal book to be engrossed in Parchment; and the Acts, Judgements and Standing Orders of the House be enrolled and kept in Parchment." Before 1621 the records of the Lords, now in the care of the Record Office of the House, are relatively few in number, but from 1621 onwards they document very thoroughly the peers' daily proceedings.

It is thus of particular interest that it should be in this same year that we first have mention of the use of part of the Jewel Tower for housing the records of Parliament. This occurs in a note of the payment of £6 to one Thomas Hicks, "Brickleyour, for making and turning over a vaulte of brickes in the Roome where the Recordes of Parliament are kept, xiiij foote long and xij foote wide and a bricke in thickness, finding Brickes Lyme and Sand and workmanshipp, with digging into the walles for the setting of the Arche and finishing the same vaulte with finishing morter." The room in question is the small inner room on the first floor of the tower (page 25-26), and the brick vault, the only one in the building, still exists. The purpose of providing it with a vault in place of its former wooden ceiling was to make it fire-proof. As a further precaution against fire it was also given an iron door, on which the royal cipher I:R: and the date 1621 appropriately commemorate the beginning of this new chapter in the Jewel Tower's fortunes.

A famous incident that took place twenty years later, at the time of Charles I's attempted arrest of the Five Members, has been previously, but probably wrongly, associated with the Jewel Tower. The story of what happened can best be told in the words of John Rushworth who, after the King, was the principal participant:

The same evening his Majesty sent James Maxwell, Usher of the House of Peers, to the House of Commons to require Mr Rushworth, the Clerk Assistant, whom his Majesty had observed to take his Speech in characters (i.e. shorthand) at the Table in the House, to come to his Majesty. And when Maxwell brought him to the King, his majesty Commanded him to give him a Copy of his Speech in the House, Mr Rushworth humbly besought his Majesty (hoping for an excuse) to call to mind how Mr Francis Nevil, a Yorkshire Member of the House of Commons, was committed to the Tower but for telling his Majesty what words were spoken in the House by Mr Henry Bellasis, sonne to the Lord Faulconbridge, to which his Majesty smartly replied, I do not ask you to tell me what was said by any Member of the House but what I said my self. Whereupon he readily gave Obedience to his Majesties Command, and in his Majesties presence in the room called the Jewel House he Transcribed his Majesties Speech out of his Characters, his Majesty staying in the Room all the while. And then and there presented the same to the King, which his Majesty was pleased to command to be sent speedily to the Press, and the next morning it came forth in Print.

Naturally enough, the coincidence that the former Jewel Tower in the Palace of Westminster was this time a repository for parliamentary records has led to its being assumed to have been the scene of the Clerk Assistant's interview. But Rushworth was summoned to the King and not vice-versa, and it would thus almost certainly have been in the "secrete Juel house" in Whitehall Palace, whence

Old Palace Yard, Westminster, c1720, with the Jewel Tower on the extreme left. Drawing by Leonard Knyff (1650-1722), reproduced by courtesy of the Trustees of the British Museum

the King had come that afternoon to the Commons, and not in "Tholde Juel-house" at Westminster, that Charles made Rushworth transcribe his shorthand notes of what His Majesty had said.

By the time of the Restoration, we find that the tower, with a house adjacent to it, is the accepted home of the records of the House of Lords. In April 1660, Henry Scobell, Clerk of the House of Commons under the Commonwealth, who had evidently retained some of the records in his private charge, was ordered to restore to John Browne, the dispossessed Clerk of the Parliaments, "possession of a certain Stone Building, standing within the Dwelling House in the Old Palace at Westminster belonging to the Clerk of the Parliaments who attends as Clerk to the House of Peers, called The Tower, wherein the Records

were usually kept, and the keys and other things belonging to the same, As also the Acts, Ordinances, Journals, Records &c." The dwelling house here referred to was the predecessor, and stood on part of the site, of the present numbers 6 and 7 Old Palace Yard, build as a residence for the Clerk and offices for his staff in 1754 (page 18).

Archaeological evidence recovered in the course of clearance work carried out during 1954-55 showed that it was about this time that the moat round the outside of the tower was filled in. A record of 5 May 1664, printed in the House of Lords' Journals, supports this:

Upon Report made by the Earl of Bridgwater (who, with other Lords (calling to their assistance Sir John Denham, Surveyor General of His Majesty's Works), have

Estimate for repairs and works at the Jewel Tower, dated March 1716, and bearing the signatures of Sir Christopher Wren (then aged 83 and in his thirty-eighth year as the Surveyor-General of HM Works), Sir John Vanbrugh (Comptroller) and Charles Dartiquenave (Paymaster). Reproduced by kind permission of the Keeper of the Records, House of Lords Record Office, from HL Misc Papers, Parlt Office pps 409(a)

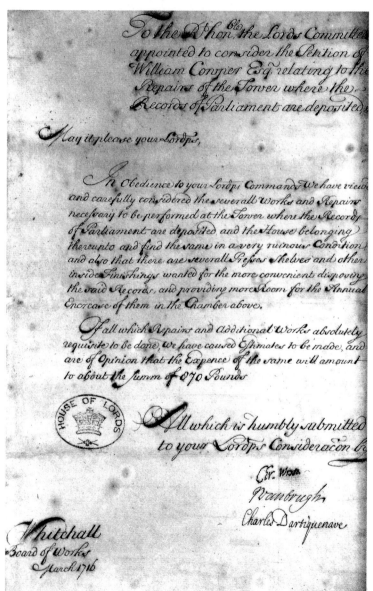

Estimate of severall Repairs and Additional Works proposed to be done at the Parliament Office. Viz

1. **Mason.** For repairing the round Stairs Battlement Stone Windows Pavings Copeings & Chimney peices — 150 . 0 . 0
2. **Bricklayer.** For making new vaulting in the upper Story, Repairing Parapets, Garden Walls, Chimneys and Pavings — 90 . 0 . 0
3. **Carpenter.** For repairing the Roofs, Gutters Partition Rough Boarding & making Scaffolds — 76 . 0 . 0
4. **Plasterer.** For rendering Lathing and Plastering whiting and mending of Ceilings — 38 . 0 . 0
5. **Plumber.** For new Casting and laying the Roof Gutters and making new Stacks of Pipes — 50 . 0 . 0
6. **Joyner.** For making severall new Wainscot Press, Shelves and Desks — 309 . 0 . 0
7. **Ironmonger.** For Locks, hinges, Bolts, nails, Screws Scutcheons — 45 . 0 . 0
8. **Smith.** For Iron Doors, Iron Windows, Casements Bolts Barrs and Strapps and screws — 60 . 0 . 0
9. **Glazier.** For repairing & new Glazing the Windows — 7 . 0 . 0
10. **Painter.** For painting the Iron Doors Windows & other outside Woodwork to preserve it — 10 . 0 . 0
11. **Labourers.** For carrying off Rubbish — 15 . 0 . 0
12. **Allowed** for accidents — 20 . 0 . 0

£ — 870

Vanbrugh
Charles Dartiquenave

viewed the Ditch, or Common Sewer,
adjoining close to the Tower where the Records
of Parliament are kept, and the House
wherein the Clerk of the Parliaments lives),
That their Lordships do find, That part of the
said Common Sewer and Ditch hath of late
been stopped up, and that the filling up of the
Remainder thereof will be an Annoyance to
the King's said House, and may endanger the
Security of the Records there kept, by making
them more liable to the Danger of Fire, and
the easier Access of Thieves:
It is thereupon ORDERED, by the Lords
Spiritual and Temporal in Parliament
assembled, that it be, and is hereby,
recommended to Mr Surveyor General of His
Majesty's Works, and to the Commissioners
for the Sewers of Westm. that they do take a
speedy and effectual Course, that the said
Common Sewer be opened as formerly it was,
whereby the Water from The Thames may
flow in and cleanse the said Common Sewer,
which is now in Part stopped up, that it
cannot flow in as usually heretofore it did;
and also to prevent any Building upon the
said Common Sewer for the future.

We do not know the outcome. The Lords
may well have been successful in securing
the cleansing of the ditch between the
tower and the river, which, as we saw
earlier, was not new when the tower was
built in 1365-66. But, if we may judge
from the contents of the filling, the moat
round the tower itself was "stopped up"
during the mid-seventeenth century and
not again reopened.

We are now approaching the time when
the Jewel Tower, at any rate externally,
was shorn of its main medieval
characteristics - mullioned and cusped
windows, moulded drip-stones,
battlements and gargoyles - and given the
curiously heterogeneous appearance that
it has today. The change was heralded by
a petition lodged by the Clerk of the
Parliaments in 1716, the year in which, as

we now know, the tower reached its three
hundred and fiftieth anniversary. He
complained that it was in a "ruinous
condition...in respect of injuries due to
weather and otherwise, and that the
officers of HM Works cannot, as they
allege, do any work beyond a certain rate
of expense without a special order". A
committee was appointed to view the
tower, and reported "that, for preserving
the records there deposited, it is
absolutely necessary the same should be
speedily repaired: that the two rooms
where the Records are at present kept are
so full, as not to be capable of containing
any more; but that there are two empty
rooms over these rooms, of the like
dimensions, where divers of the records
and papers below, for which no
convenient room remains, as also those
Yearly increasing, may very conveniently
and safely be deposited as soon as the
said empty rooms are put into a condition
for receiving them."

The Officers of the Works estimated the
cost of the necessary repairs and
alterations at £870 (pages 14 and 15),
and order was given to proceed. The work
was initiated by Hawksmoor, but owing
to his ill health and, in 1718, his dismissal
from the Surveyor Generalship, progress
was slow. By the end of that year the two
topmost rooms had been put "into a
pretty good condition for the reception of
the records, but the one of the lower ones
was not yet so much as flower'd nor
anything but Stone Work in the windows
done, and that the Windows in either of
the lower rooms were not Glaz'd, nor any
Conveniency made for the writing of the
Clerks." The estimate was already
exceeded, and because of this the brick
vaults which it was proposed to substitute
for the 1365-66 timber roofs were not
built. When the Officers of the Works
were asked if the repair was as good
without the vaults as with them, they

answered, "Not, in case of fire." How true! Their opinion was to be confirmed in May 1941, when the roof was severely damaged by German incendiary bombs.

By April 1719, the committee was able to report that "of late such a Progress has been made, & is daily making, in said Repairs, that the same will be entirely perfected in a short Time." Among further things to be done, their lordships "gave particular directions for the speedy fitting up of the little Room on the First Floor, for keeping the Journals only: And considering that a Fire would be not only convenient, but necessary, to be kept during the cold and damp season of the Year; especially in regard the Lords themselves might often have Occasion to peruse the Journals there; the committee directed a Chimney to be made in the said Room." And the committee suggested that a "reasonable Quantity of Coals and Candles may be supplied, to be used in the said Room where the Journals only are kept, as also the Rooms adjacent, where the Clerks write, and the other Records are kept, in the Tower of the said Office." We have to remember, in judging these provisions, that the printing of the Lords' Journals was only begun in 1771, and that prior to this - and indeed in many respects long afterwards - all searching of records had to be by resort to the original books and papers kept here in the Jewel Tower in conditions of congestion and discomfort that are not difficult to imagine; and in the same conditions the Clerks had likewise to compile the records of current sessions and committees.

By the time the works were finished, in September 1719, their cost had mounted to some £1118. Their effect was to leave the external appearance of the tower much as we now see it (front cover), with brick parapets having flat caps of Portland stone, round-headed windows with Portland stone dressings, and heavy iron window frames which no doubt let in a lot more light than their medieval predecessors. The heaviest single item in the account is £321 to Benjamin Jackson, the master mason, and it is to him that we should probably attribute the most conspicuous feature of the work, namely the new windows.

Despite all that had been accomplished, further improvements were called for in 1725. Another committee viewed the office in the Jewel Tower and "also the House belonging to the said Office called the King's House" and reported that they "found the room in the said office where the Acts of Parliament are deposited, not at all commodious or convenient for the proper placing and keeping of the said Acts, so as the same may be easily and readily found." The Officers of the Works were accordingly called in once more to prepare plans of every floor and a section of the whole building. They advised "that the uppermost room, where the said Acts are kept, may be made secure from Fire, by bringing up a brick Wall betwixt it and the room where the Clerks write; by making an Iron Door and Iron Window Shutters, and securing the roof; and then whatever conveniences shall be requisite therein may be made securely." These recommendations were carried into effect during 1726 at a cost of £508 15 4d, and when the committee visited the tower in 1728 they were at last able to report that the Journals, Acts of Parliament and other books and papers "are now placed and kept in the Greatest order and safety imaginable."

The question of the repair of the King's House was left in abeyance, to be revived in 1753. Though it is with the Jewel Tower itself that we are here principally concerned, the transformation that was now about to overtake the dwelling house associated with it at least since the time of

Sir Richard Shelley's tenure in the sixteenth century nevertheless has a proper claim on our attention particularly as the building which replaced it, known today as numbers 6 and 7 Old Palace Yard, has outlived, with the Jewel Tower, all the other buildings which until the last war obscured this corner of the palace site. After the long postponement, the matter was now handled with commendable expedition. On 2 February 1753, on a petition from Ashley Cowper, Esq., Clerk of the Parliaments, that "the House belonging to the Parliament office is become very ruinous and almost uninhabitable," the Lords ordered "that the Officers of His Majesty's Board of Works do survey the state and condition of The Parliament-office, and the house thereto belonging, and lay an Account of the same before this House. Fourteen days later Henry Flitcroft, Master Mason and Deputy Surveyor of the Works, attended in person at the Bar of the House and delivered the Board's report, which, after due interval, was formally read on 14 March. Of the Jewel Tower itself, the officers reported that the vaulted ground-floor rooms had "been used for a Kitchen and Scullery; which, they apprehend, should not be there, but added to The Parliament-office." They continued, nevertheless, to be so used until 1864. With regard to the King's House adjoining, the officers found this to be "an old Timber Building; and so ruinous, that they think it not advisable to lay out any Money to repair it." The Lords thereupon ordered a humble address to His Majesty "to direct such repairs to the Parliament-Office as were necessary and to re-build the House belonging thereto," and on 21 March the King was pleased to say he would order accordingly.

The erection of the new "Apartments for the Clerk of the Parliament and his Assistants in Palace Yard Westminster" was authorised by Treasury Warrant of 10 July 1754. The work was duly completed, at a cost of £2432, by November of the following year. The design has been attributed to John Vardy. The surviving accounts record no payment to him however, and just before building was begun he left Westminster to become Clerk of Works at Kensington. On the whole there is perhaps more to be said for an ascription to Flitcroft's lifelong protege Kenton Couse, whom the accounts name as Clerk of Works for the building and who received a fee of ten guineas "for Measuring, making out Bills and Adjusting the Accompts."

The Parliament Office consisted from now on of two more or less distinct parts, with the accumulated records - Acts, Journals, Minute Books and a score of other categories - preserved in the Jewel Tower, and the Clerk of the Parliaments and his office staff housed in the building of 1754. A further house, in Abingdon Street, was added to the complex in 1792. The Record Commissioners reported in 1800 that they found the records in the Jewel Tower in good preservation and methodically kept and arranged. In 1826, Soane prepared proposals for additional storage and, although the Parliament Office itself was transferred to new premises two years later, the Rolls of Parliament continued to be kept in the Jewel Tower. But the great fire of 1834 prepared the way for changes which were to affect the buildings that escaped it no less than those it consumed. As the new Houses of Parliament rose on the other side of Old Palace Yard, accommodation was reallocated and in due course the Clerk of the Parliaments migrated to the new premises. In 1864 the older records of Parliament followed and were housed after this in the recently completed Victoria Tower, which must have seemed at the time to offer almost unlimited scope for their expansion. It was an appropriate rearrangement, linking by usage the newest and the oldest towers of the Palace of Westminster.

1869-1938 Weights and Measures Office

An Act of Parliament passed two years later, that is to say just 500 years after the Jewel Tower was built, opened the way for what was to be the final phase of its active life. Almost from time immemorial the Exchequer, one of our oldest organs of government, had numbered among its functions that of maintaining and ensuring the country-wide application of the English standard measures of length, weight and capacity, as for instance the imperial yard or imperial pint which go back to origins that are lost in the mists of antiquity. But, from the earliest times of which we have record, there were kept at Westminster "standards" from which all other weights and measures theoretically derived and against which they could, ultimately, be balanced and tested.

The Act of 1866 transferred these functions of standardising, balancing and testing from the Exchequer to the Board of Trade. The Board's Standards Department, directed by the Warden of the Standards, was thereupon established in the Clerk of the Parliaments' former quarters at Old Palace Yard, while preparations were made to accommodate the standard measures themselves and the elaborate testing equipment used in connection with them in the adjoining Jewel Tower.

The tower was occupied for its new purposes in 1869. At that time, because of the great thickness of its stone walls, it was regarded as "very favourable for standard operations, being free from vibration and not liable to sudden fluctuations of temperature." On the ground floor the large vaulted chamber was fitted up as the weighing room, the small inner room housing the glass fluid measures and their associated comparator apparatus. The first-floor rooms were given over to the standards of length, also with their equivalent apparatus. Finally, on the top floor, space was found for the large collection of older standards of an antiquarian or historical character, some of them going back to the time of Henry VII (1485-1509). "The old roof of these upper rooms," runs the Warden's annual report for 1869-70," with its large beams of chestnut wood, has been completely restored by the Office of Works, after considerable difficulties were overcome from its decayed state." It was this roof of Hugh Herland's, let it be remembered, that the Office of Works had wanted to replace with brick vaulting as far back as 1718 (page 16).

In the course of the next half-century the work of the Standards Department greatly expanded, not only on account of the development of new scientific media and techniques but also in relation to the vastly increased territories, virtually embracing all the lands of the Commonwealth, which look to it for primary guidance in matters within its competence. In the years between the wars it became increasingly clear that the Jewel Tower, the condition of the structure of which was then also beginning to give cause for serious concern, could not be expected to meet demands put upon it for very much longer.

In 1931 the ancient standards were removed from the top floor and transferred to the Science Museum at South Kensington, where the majority of them are now displayed. Shortly afterwards, changes effected in Abingdon Street, following the opening, in July

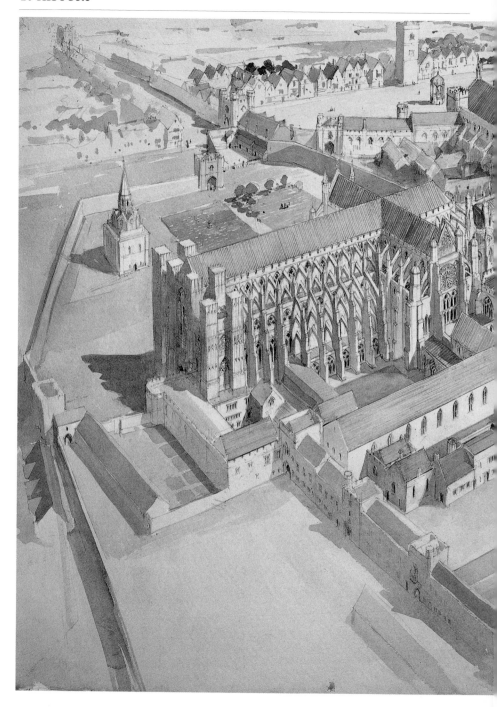

A bird's eye view of the Jewel Tower and the Palace of Westminster as it may have appeared in around 1510.

1932, of the new Lambeth Bridge, introduced new and deciding factors. The resulting great increase in the speed, weight and volume of passing traffic caused so much vibrations as to render it difficult to conduct any precision work except in the ground-floor rooms, which were in any case being found less well adapted for the purpose. The same causes also further weakened the fabric, which showed increasing signs of settlement. Accordingly, in May 1938, the Standards Department, or, as it is often called, the Weights and Measures Testing Department, vacated both the Jewel Tower and the Clerk of the Parliaments' House and transferred to new premises in Chapter Street, Westminster.

Epilogue
The Jewel Tower as an historic monument

After the Second World War, the Jewel Tower was not reoccupied. Instead, it was put into sound repair and now, after close on six centuries of royal, parliamentary and scientific service, it is maintained and cherished as a national monument. Difficult and complex conservation works were carried out between 1948 and 1959, and the building and its surroundings freed from a cluster of disfiguring later additions.

Serious fracturing of the main walls necessitated the underpinning of the tower and the removal from beneath it of the wooded piles on which the fourteenth-century foundations were laid. The walls themselves were strengthened with concealed reinforcements, grouted and pointed. The parapets were reset and defective stones replaced. Within, many stonework defects were made good and a number of the later blockings and intrusions removed, so that the rooms are now essentially the medieval chambers as modified in 1621 and by Hawksmoor, Flitcroft and Kenton Couse in the eighteenth century. The stairs between the ground and first floors, taken out in the eighteenth or early nineteenth century, were reinstated and the head of the entrance doorway renewed.

At the top of the building the medieval timber roofs had to be largely renewed following extensive damage by fire in the air raids of 1941. The repairs carried out in 1864-69 (page 25) had proved ineffective, and in the 1920s the main timbers had had to be suspended from superimposed steel girders. These were now removed and the roofs carefully reframed so as to retain the form and, so far as their condition allowed, the substance of the medieval originals.

Removal of later buildings surrounding the Jewel Tower allowed the moat to be re-opened and a small garden, recalling the little close formed round it when it was built, to be laid out. Some of the stones used in repairing the moat revetment walls came from the Tudor river-wall of Whitehall Palace discovered and demolished in preparing the site of the present Ministry of Defence building between Whitehall and the Embankment just before the War. As a result of all these various works, carried out for the most part in the 1950s and completed with the laying out of the new Abingdon Street Garden in 1965, we may visualise, at least to some extent, as we look upon the scene today, the setting of Edward III's Jewel Tower in the years of its prime.

Description

Exterior

As we approach the door of the Jewel Tower from the junction of Abingdon Street and Old Palace Yard, we find ourselves, quite literally, in what the fourteenth-century documents called "the angle of the private palace" *(in angulo privati palacii)*. The angle is formed by two sides of the Jewel Tower itself, the tower being L-shaped on plan. A glance at the outer ends of these sides shows that for some way up from the ground, instead of being finely edged, they are ragged and broken. This is because, originally, both of them were prolonged, northwards and eastwards respectively, to form the west and south boundary walls of the palace. The broken ends show where these walls have been torn away.

From the angle there can be seen, through the gap on the right between the tower and the back of numbers 6 and 7, Old Palace Yard (page 17), the deep water-filled moat which, beginning at this point, originally bounded the south side of the medieval palace all the way to the river. As we have seen (page 7), the moat was part of the original layout of the tower; it was designed to protect it against fire and perhaps also against a repetition of the notorious burglary of the royal treasure from the crypt of the nearby Abbey Chapter House in 1303. Round the sides of the moat was a little garden (page 5), now laid out as lawns; it is bounded on the south and west by the Abbey precinct wall, the building of which there is reason to believe marked the first stage in the laying out of the Jewel Tower site in 1364-65. At the same time the main drain of the Abbey was diverted to a new south-easterly course aligned to run just clear of the corner of the moat (see the plan at end of this handbook).

The tower itself is a three-storey building, with one large and one small room on each floor and a projecting stair-turret on the north. The main walls of Kentish rag, though much patched and repaired, are original work of 1365-66. Until 1954 they rested on their old foundation of close-set elm piles driven into the clay and gravel sub-soil and capped with horizontal sleepers of oak. A reinforced concrete foundation has been substituted. Most of the windows are early eighteenth-century reconstructions of medieval predecessors (page 17). Among the exceptions are the two lowest windows on the south side, both of which are new insertions of the same period. Originally, for greater security, there were no ground-floor windows facing south or west, while those at the upper levels on these sides were only of single-light width. On the other hand each of the three larger rooms had what was originally a great two-light window looking out on to the relative safety of the palace garden. No doubt these were the three windows for which large iron grilles were provided in 1365, but the reconstruction of 1718 has removed all trace of them. The flat-topped parapets and stair-head likewise date from 1718 and replace the battlemented tops of the fourteenth century.

Ground Floor

The tower is entered from the site of the palace garden through a restored eighteenth-century doorway which leads to a lobby at the foot of the stairs. A door on the left of the lobby opens into the larger of the two ground-floor rooms. This is a fine vaulted chamber, the roof of which is divided into two bays, with hollow-chamfered main, medial and ridge ribs springing from octagonal wall-shafts with moulded caps and bases. The carved bosses include one with a group of grotesque heads above a triple rose, another with three intertwined birds, and a third having four grimacing faces with their wide-opened mouths meeting in a quatrefoil (page 29). The tall embrasure near the door, now containing a modern oak-framed window, retains its medieval dressings, though the right-hand splay has

been hacked back to give greater width for the insertion of the iron-framed window of 1718. Until then its fourteenth-century predecessor, mullioned and probably transomed, and containing heraldic glass (page 7), gave the room its only light. The wall opposite contained a fireplace with hooded chimney-piece. The hood was removed in the eighteenth century and in the repairs of the 1950s the fireplace itself, spoiled in successive mutilations, was blocked up. The window in the south wall is a modern replacement of what was most probably an eighteenth-century insertion: the rough edges of the embrasure contrast markedly with those of the fourteenth-

Ground floor. Left: View of principal room looking south-east
Above: Roof bosses in principal ground-floor room

century opening already noted. The original floor was of red Flanders tiles about 1ft square.

A door in the east wall leads directly into the smaller room, likewise vaulted in stone with hollow-chamfered diagonal and wall-ribs springing from similar octagonal shafts. The original window was on the north, looking over the garden; in its present form it represents an eighteenth-century enlargement of what was probably a medieval single light. The window opposite is an eighteenth-century insertion. The recess in the east wall originally contained a garderobe or latrine discharging directly into the moat.

These two rooms form what was clearly designed as the principal suite of the building. The larger may be identified with confidence as Sleaford's office in his capacity as Keeper of the Privy Wardrobe and Clerk of the Jewels and Vessels of Gold and Silver within the King's Private Palace, the smaller as a retiring room attached to it. So long as the tower served its original purpose, both are likely to have been so occupied by his successors. They never, strictly speaking, became part of the Parliament Office, which from 1621 to 1718 occupied only the middle and thereafter the middle and top floors of the tower. Instead they were used - most unsuitably, as the Office of Works observed in 1753 - as the kitchen and scullery of adjoining premises. As late as 1863 we read that the antiquary who wished to see what was worth seeing in the Jewel Tower might do so by explaining that the part he desired to visit was "the basement or kitchen occupied by Mrs Vincent, the housekeeper, and that he does not wish to go into the Record tower itself; in which there is nothing for him to see, so far as the architecture is concerned, all vestiges of antiquity having been carefully destroyed." On at least one occasion this "basement or kitchen" was

flooded. According to a record of January 1690, "the Parliament-office is now, and for these Two Months has hath been, very much annoyed and damnified by Water coming into the Rooms under the said Office, which may very much prejudice the Records there, and doth endanger them, for that the lower Doors of the said Office or Tower cannot be shut." The two ground floor rooms now contain an exhibition about the history of Parliament which continues on the upper floors. Also displayed are a sword, dating from around 800 AD found in Victoria Tower Gardens, eight late eleventh century capitals from William Rufus' Westminster Hall and some of the wooden piles on which the Jewel Tower was originally built.

First Floor

The first sixteen steps of the staircase leading to the upper floors are replacements, inserted in 1952, of medieval originals removed at some unknown date in the eighteenth or early nineteenth century. For many years it had been possible to reach the upper storeys only by a door from an adjoining building (now demolished) broken through the eastern window-opening of the smaller first-floor room.

The main first-floor room is entered directly from the stair by a doorway with shouldered head and rear-arch and hollow-chamfered jambs. Its eighteenth-century door retains a fine iron bolt of the period. The arrangement follows that below, with the main light coming from the direction of the former palace garden. On the left of the entrance is a great iron-framed window of 1718 with opening casement, set in the embrasure of its two-light medieval predecessor. Opposite to it is the fireplace, robbed of its hood in the seventeenth or eighteenth century. In the north-west corner, in the same wall as the door, there is an inserted eighteenth-century single-light window, now blocked and only visible from the outside of the building. The small window facing the door is the successor to a medieval original and has a well-preserved fourteenth-century embrasure with pointed head. The openings to the right of it, however, one in the south and one in the west wall (now a cupboard) are eighteenth- (possibly original seventeenth-) century insertions, made to give more light in the period when this was the writing room of the record clerks. The stone-vaulted ceiling dates from the eighteenth century, belonging in all probability to the year 1753, when the accounts record payment of £350 for unspecified works at the Parliament Office. The timber-framed ceiling which it replaced would then have been nearly 400 years old.

As originally built, the division between the larger and the smaller room, both on this floor and on the floor above, consisted of a wooden partition or screen framed at the top into a wall-plate dividing the two parts of the ceiling. Both screens, for the making of which (together with doors and window shutters) a contractor, Richard Burnham, was paid £2 16s 8d in 1366, were subsequently replaced by brick walls, and in each case the junction of the brick against the original stonework is readily noticed. On this floor, as the date on the little inserted iron door shows, the change had already been made by 1621.

The smaller room was originally lit both from the garden side and from the east, the south window (behind the door) being an insertion of uncertain, perhaps seventeenth-century, date. As on the other floors there is a recess for a garderobe, converted into a fireplace in 1719 but now restored. The barrel vault, of brick covered with plaster, was substituted for the original wooden ceiling in 1621. The

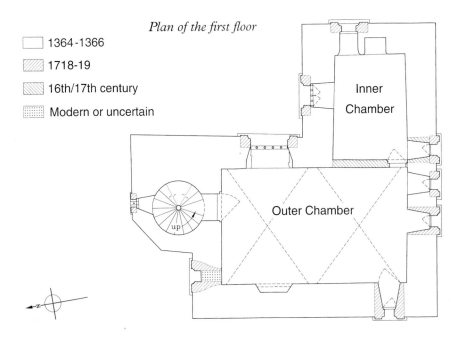

Plan of the first floor

☐ 1364-1366

▨ 1718-19

▧ 16th/17th century

▦ Modern or uncertain

Inner Chamber

Outer Chamber

up

iron shutter is the only survivor of those fitted generally to the upper-floor windows in 1719 and 1726.

It was on this floor, both in the Jewel House and in the Parliament Office period, that the real work of the building was carried on. If, in the former days, we are right in assigning the more sumptuous ground-floor chambers to the Keeper of the Privy Wardrobe, we may reasonably suppose this middle floor to have been occupied by the clerk who, if Tower of London practice was followed, conducted the routine business of the office on his behalf. Again, when early in the seventeenth century the Parliament records came to the tower, we have seen that to begin with it was in the little inner first-floor room that they were lodged, while the clerks who laboriously compiled or copied them toiled outside it in the larger room. Not until 1719 did the record accumulations of a century finally burst their bounds and spread to the rooms above. Among the exhibits on this floor are examples of the Speaker's state robe and everyday dress.

Second Floor

The stairs continue to the second or top floor of the tower and thence to the leads. As on the first floor, a doorway with bold shouldered lintel opens directly into the larger room, but between this doorway and the one below there is a notable difference: for greater security it is rebated for double doors. The outer door has gone. The inner remains and will repay careful inspection. It is of eight lapped panels, cross-framed and heavily studded, and is hung from two strap hinges with the gudgeons set tightly to the jamb. The lock panel is inserted, but otherwise the whole door, with its iron handle and six-lobbed latch-knob, has all the appearance of being the original fourteenth-century fitting.

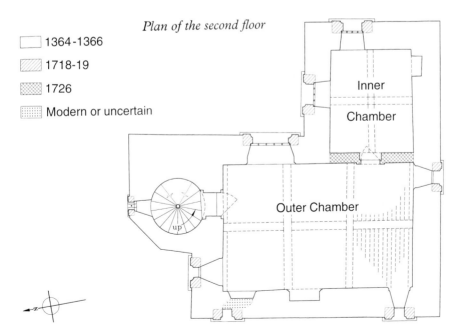

Plan of the second floor

☐ 1364-1366

▨ 1718-19

▧ 1726

▨ Modern or uncertain

Inner
Chamber

Outer Chamber

up

Following the pattern of the lower floors, the east wall has the embrasure of a medieval two-light window, replaced by the present iron-framed one in 1719, while opposite to it there is an original fireplace. Three smaller windows, one in each of the other walls, are eighteenth-century replacements of medieval single lights. All retain their fourteenth-century embrasures, which it will be noted are rebated for shutters to be fitted flush with the wall - a feature found on this floor alone. Beside the fireplace there are the reveals of a fourth medieval embrasure, now blocked, but showing eighteenth-century dressings externally. The brick wall separating the outer and inner rooms dates from 1726, and the "gothic" doorcase of Portland stone, framing a heavy iron door, is an interesting attempt by the eighteenth century Office of Works to reflect the medieval character of the building. Both the windows of the inner room are in medieval embrasures, which, like those in the adjoining chamber, were originally rebated for wall shutters. There is also a recess corresponding to those in the rooms below. The roofs of both rooms are modern replicas of the originals, most of the timbers of which were too badly charred for re-use after the war-damage of 1941; the greater part of the main beam nearest the staircase and a portion of the next main beam are, however, original.

It was a common medieval practice to place private treasuries and muniment rooms at the tops of towers. Whereas today we seek our surest shelter below ground, in those times a high stone tower gave the best protection against robbery and the fire of the enemy. There is little doubt that the Jewel Tower followed custom in this respect and that, at any rate when it was first built, most if not all of its valuables were stored in these topmost rooms. The probability that this was so is borne out both by the provision of double doors from the staircase and the fitting of shutters to the five smaller window embrasures, which could thereby be converted into wall cupboards. Nevertheless the presence, as on the lower floors, of the usual fireplace and wall recess, shows that this floor, like the others, was designed to be used not merely as a passive repository but also as somebody's office. Here then, perhaps, when he attended, sat the yeoman of the Privy Wardrobe, who would be personally responsible, like his opposite number at the Tower of London, for seeing to the "trewe and diligent kepinge of the foresayd jewelles" (page 8).

What happened to these rooms in the years before their eventual absorption by the Parliament Office we do not know. Afterwards, as we have seen, they housed the ancient Exchequer standards - by no means inappropriate successors to gold and silver vessels whose value was habitually expressed in terms of their measure by weight. Now, no less appropriately, they are given over to the display of exhibits including some of the former standards which illustrate the story of the tower itself and of the palaces of Westminster and Whitehall.